CONTENTS

- 4 From rulers to relics
- 6 Meet the beast
- 8 Stone or bone?
- 10 Dinosaurs uncovered
- 12 My epic adventure
- 14 In the footsteps of dinosaurs
- 16 Spotter's guide
- 18 Yaverland safari
- 19 Fox safari
- 20 Dinosaur map
- 22 Footprint safari
- 23 Needles safari
- 24 Dino plant safari
- 26 Famous hunters
- 28 Virtual dinosaurs
- 30 Dinodraw
- 32 Epic activities: are you a geekosaurus?
- 33 Spot the difference
- 34 Wordsearch
- 35 Activities answers
- 36 Meet Jurassic Jim
- 37 Dino discounts

VOUCHERS WORTH OVER £17

- 38 The end... or is it the beginning?

ISLE OF WIGHT Official Dinosaur Safari Guide

WELCOME FELLOW HUNTER

I remember the first dinosaur I ever met, a Brontosaurus in the American Museum of Natural History. It was 150 million years old, I was just five.

I came home and learnt everything I could about these 'terrible lizards' – that's what 'dinosaurs' means! Fast forward 50 years, and I moved to the Isle of Wight, where dinosaurs roamed 130 million years ago. This is the UK's dinosaur capital and one of the best places in the world to find fossils. I started taking groups of school children on dinosaur safaris. To do my research, I visited every dinosaur-related museum, shop and beach on the Island, met lots of interesting people, took hundreds of photos and collected my own set of dinosaur fossils. I read every book and watched all the movies. But I discovered that there has never been a dinosaur handbook for the Island. That's when the idea of an Isle of Wight Official Dinosaur Safari Guide came to me – the first one in 130 million years.

I hope you enjoy reading it and have fun exploring Dinosaur Island!

Steve Love
Author & dinosaur hunter

DAISY'S TIPS

Hello, I'm **Daisy Morris** and when I was four, I found a fossil on Atherton Beach that turned out to be a new species of flying pterosaur. It was named Vectidraco daisymorrisae – the first part of the name means Isle of Wight dragon, the second part was named after me! It's fun to go down to the beach and you never know what you'll find next... maybe you'll discover a new species too. My special tips for you are in this Guide. Good luck!

Love Daisy x

DIANA SAW'S SCOOP!

I'm **Diana Saw** – your roving reporter. Look out for my sensational scoops in your Official Dinosaur Safari Guide. I've got an 'access all areas' pass to the Isle of Wight... and I'm gonna use it!

FROM RULERS...

Neovenator, a top predator of the early Cretaceous period, found on the Isle of Wight.

1. IN THE BEGINNING...
130 million years ago, where the Island now stands, there used to be a large fertile low-lying plain with rivers, lagoons and plants. The wildlife included dinosaurs, crocodiles, turtles and flying lizards.

2. FLASH FLOODS
The climate was generally hot and dry, but occasional violent floods swept up everything in their path – plants, trees, pebbles, sand, mud, dung, teeth, bones and sometimes complete animals.

3. DINOS DUMPED
This debris was dumped as the water levels went back to normal. The vegetation rotted first, and the chemical processes that occurred helped to preserve the bones.

Explore the Island with visitisleofwight.co.uk. This picture was taken at Compton.

DINOSAUR ISLAND ROCKS!

If you've been to the Natural History Museum in London, you will have seen their magnificent skeletons of dinosaurs from world-famous sites in the USA, Canada and South Africa – Tyrannosaurus, Stegosaurus, Triceratops and the like.

TIMELINE

Jurassic era - 210m years ago
Giant dinosaurs ruled the earth (but not on the Isle of Wight).

Cretaceous era - 145m years ago
Cretaceous come from the Greek work 'creta' meaning 'chalk'. Most chalk was formed during this period from the skeletons of microscopic sea creatures.

Dinosaurs roamed the Isle of Wight (140m to 115m years ago). They were wiped out as the sea levels rose.

Other dinos around the world lived on for another 55m years. They probably became extinct when a giant asteroid hit the earth.

ISLE OF WIGHT Official Dinosaur Safari Guide

...TO RELICS

Iguanodon skeleton at Dinosaur Isle, dating back 125 million years.

4 FOSSILISATION
Some bones turned into white stone, as they absorbed calcium carbonate in the water. Others turned black as they lay in iron-rich mud and the iron replaced minerals in the bones.

5 SWALLOWED BY SEA
Around 115 million years ago, the sea rose up and covered the plain. When the sea creatures died, their remains were preserved in the sandstone and chalk on the seabed.

6 THE GREAT REVEAL
Much later, movement of the earth's crust threw up a great fold of rock where the Isle of Wight now stands, with the chalky 'sea bed' on top and the dinosaur beds below.

Among them, there is a spectacular specimen that has come all the way from the Isle of Wight – a magnificent and complete Iguanodon.

To dinosaur hunters, this is no surprise, because they know that the Isle of Wight is one of the best places for dinosaurs *in the world*. That's why it's known as Dinosaur Island.

The fossils here mostly date from the Cretaceous ('chalk') era that began 145 million years ago. The best known dinosaurs, including Tyrannosaurus rex, Triceratops, Stegosaurus and the Island's Iguanodons come from this period.

Nearly 200 years ago, some of the world's very first dinosaur finds were discovered here. Since then, over 20 types of dinosaur have been found on the Island, more than at almost any other site in the world. Fossils of their bones, teeth, skeletons, footprints (pictured) and food are all preserved here. Some dinosaurs have *only* been found on the Isle of Wight and nowhere else in the world. And they are still being found today. So what are you waiting for? Get hunting!

Palaeogene era - 60m years ago
Mammals evolved and many new types emerged including primates (our early ancestors) and birds that you would recognise today. The weather became cooler and drier.

Neogene era - 23m years ago
Mammals and birds continued to evolve into the species we recognise today. It became colder as the Ice Age approached.

Quaternary era - 2.5m years ago
The first Ice Age.

First grass appeared.

10m years later the first flowers evolved.

Many of today's plants evolved in this era.

Caveman and mammoths evolved.

MEET THE BEAST

By John Sibbick

SUPER SCALY SKIN
Some dinosaurs had feathers – Iguanodons had scales.

THUMBS UP!

TERRIBLE TAIL
The tail was held in place by rods which ran along the Iguanodon's backbone and helped to balance the mighty weight of the dinosaur's front end.
EVIDENCE: Iguanodon skeleton with stiffening rods along its back.

TREACHEROUS THUMBS
Ouch! When the first Iguanodon remains were found, people thought the sharp, bony spike went on its nose. More complete fossils now show that it belongs on the thumb – a handy weapon against predators and rivals.
EVIDENCE: Fossilised hand with spike.

ISLE OF WIGHT Official Dinosaur Safari Guide

It's time to get up close and personal with the Iguanodon – the plant eating monster from the Isle of Wight.

Imagine stumbling on one of these creatures! You can guess how surprised the Victorians were when they started finding dinosaur skeletons on the Isle of Wight. Since then, so many more discoveries have been made that experts have built up detailed pictures of what dinosaurs looked like. So here's your guide to the body beautiful of the Iguanodon, the Island's most famous dino…

Adult Iguanodons weighed 3 tonnes and were up to 4 metres tall – that's heavier than a car and as high as a double decker bus!

BITING BEAK
To bite off tough vegetation these dinos had a huge beak. Food was sliced up by their sharp teeth, which were shaped like chisels. The upper and lower jaws slid over each other to chop up plants like a garden shredder before swallowing… gulp!
EVIDENCE: An Iguanodon jaw and beak.

AWESOME EYESIGHT
This beast had sharp, beady eyes – all the better to see you with, my dear!
EVIDENCE: No fossilised dinosaur eyes exist. But birds (which are descended from dinos) and reptiles have excellent eyesight.

BIG BAD BONES
The bones were dense and strong on the outside – but hollow or like honeycomb inside to keep the massive weight down.
EVIDENCE: We've found plenty of bones that are hollow inside. The interior of this Iguanodon leg bone has partly filled with glittering quartz crystals.

FEARSOME FEET
These giants plodded around on their big hind feet. Their feet had three toes, which spread out to take their great weight.
EVIDENCE: They thoughtfully left behind lots of footprints and footcasts for us to see at Hanover Point. Many fossils have also been found including the back foot of an Iguanodon (pictured).

BEAUTIFUL BABIES
They laid eggs in nests… which then hatched into cute little babies. Well, they looked cute to their Mummy and Daddy. These dinos lived in family groups or herds.
EVIDENCE: We can see lots of Iguanodon footprints, including big ones and small ones together. Iguanodon eggs have not been found yet, so be on full alert!

Picture taken of a reconstruction at the Natural History Museum

STONE OR BONE?

So have you found prehistoric treasure… or just another pebble? Look at the checklist below, then take the challenge and identify the finds on these pages.

A

Tick: Bone ◯ Stone ◯ Something else ◯

IS IT A BONE…

- It's usually black or very dark brown (white is rare).
- It probably has a shiny surface.
- It actually looks like a piece of broken bone that's been smoothed by the waves.
- It's hard, like rock (which it is). If it crumbles and it's light, it could be fossilised wood.
- It's heavy, because it contains a lot of iron.
- It could have a layer that looks like the inside of an Aero or Flake – that's the inner bone. The 'bubbles' could be white crystals.

Daisy's tip It's best to go fossil hunting at low tide, and after rough weather or a storm. That way you don't have to do any digging as the bad weather washes them out from the cliffs.

STONE…

- If it's not a bone, then it's probably a stone. However look closely in case there are any patterns which could indicate that it's 'something else' (see right).

STICK A PICTURE OF YOUR FAVOURITE FIND HERE

ISLE OF WIGHT Official Dinosaur Safari Guide

B Bone ○ Stone ○ Something else ○

C Bone ○ Stone ○ Something else ○

D Bone ○ Stone ○ Something else ○

E Bone ○ Stone ○ Something else ○

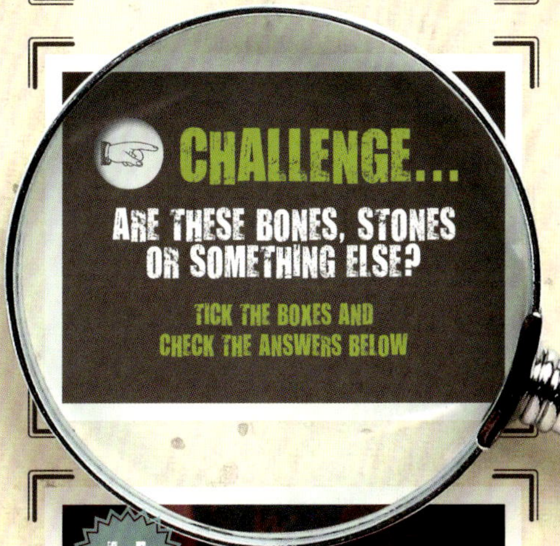

CHALLENGE...
ARE THESE BONES, STONES OR SOMETHING ELSE?
TICK THE BOXES AND CHECK THE ANSWERS BELOW

F Bone ○ Stone ○ Something else ○

G Bone ○ Stone ○ Something else ○

H Bone ○ Stone ○ Something else ○

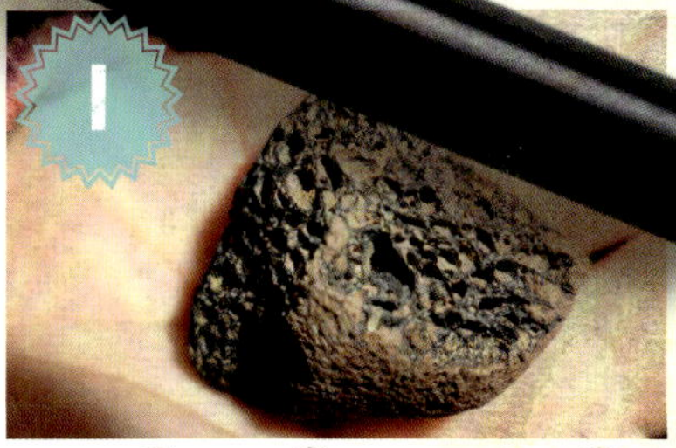

I Bone ○ Stone ○ Something else ○

...OR SOMETHING ELSE?

There's an amazing array of fossilised sealife and vegetation to be found including clams, ammonites, sponges and ancient hazelnuts.

 **Daisy's tip** Look out for round pebbles as they could be fossilised sea urchins - they are about 2.5-5cm and have a star pattern in the middle on one side.

ANSWERS

A. **Bone** – look at the distinctive texture and black colour. B. **Stone** – this is a flint and much too light in colour to be a dinosaur fossil. C. **Something else** – this is fossilised wood (you can see the grain). D. **Stone** – but this is a very special stone. It's a gastrolith which was swallowed by a dinosaur to help digestion. The giveaway is the highly polished surface. E. **Stone** – it's heavy and it looks like a giant bone but this is actually ironstone which is really common on Island beaches. F. **Something else** – this flat, grey rock is embedded with clusters of fossilised shells. G. **Stone** – it looks like coprolite (fossilised dung) but unfortunately it's just iron pyrite mineral. H. **Bone** – The shiny black surface gives it away and it looks like a bone. I. **Bone** – check out the Aero texture, plus this is heavy and black/dark brown.

WHAT TO BRING

- Sensible shoes
- Waterproof trousers or just prepare to get wet
- Camera
- Food and drink (some of the beaches don't have a café nearby).

TALK TO THE BONE BOFFINS

Take your most interesting finds to Dinosaur Isle and their experts will identify them for you (pictured). The Dinosaur Expeditions, Conservation and Palaeoart Centre at Dinosaur Farm also provides an excellent fossil identification service. All contact details are on page 38.

9

DINOSAURS UNCOVERED

Dinosaur Isle is the UK's biggest dinosaur museum. Read on, and discover the secrets behind the scenes, with ace reporter Diana Saw…

DIANA SAW'S SCOOP!

You can't miss Dinosaur Isle. It's based in a pterosaur shaped building that watches over the dinosaur coast at Sandown. The museum has just celebrated its millionth visitor since opening in 2001 – but very few people get the chance to sneak around the labs and get a guided tour from Steve Hutt, the mastermind behind it all. So this was my lucky day.

Steve led me straight to the huge skeleton of the carnivore Neovenator. "This really is the star of the museum," he told me. "It took 20 years to recover all the bones, because it was found by different people who each took some away. It is totally new to science - I had to check out every similar dinosaur in the world, to rule out a match. And it was a nightmare to assemble!"

The biggest exhibit of all is the huge Brachiosaur that fills a case from the floor to high ceiling. And guess what? Steve Hutt found it! "It was a rainy day", he recalls. "I was walking along the cliffs and slid on a muddy bit when I happened to see a tiny bit of bone. I dug around for two days and found more. In the end it took a team of us two years to dig out a huge chunk of the cliff, in mud, cold and rain. Then it took us another six years to clean and prepare it. But it was worth it."

Equally huge is the Iguanodon, the source of most of the footcasts that you will see on the Island's beaches.

Steve then takes me to see skeletons of small dinosaurs and points out a miniature Hypsilophodon. "It was found right next to a full sized one. This is a strong clue that they lived in herds or family groups."

Then we see bones of the fearsome Eotyrannus, an early relative of T-rex. "Someone walked in to our museum with a single claw, and then we all went out to help dig up the rest," says Steve, who explains that they always get permission from the landowner first.

They have a network of volunteers who are happy to help when something exciting like this is found… and their help is invaluable, particularly when it comes to swinging the pick-axe! Steve says: "It's great looking for dinosaurs, and it's fantastic actually finding them… but it's nothing but hard work to dig them up!"

110,000 year old leg bone from an elephant, found on the Isle of Wight, where they lived in warm spells between Ice Ages. It's 85cm long.

ISLE OF WIGHT Official Dinosaur Safari Guide

ROCK SHOCK!

"I use a toothbrush for the most delicate cleaning"
Gary Blackwell

Top: There are Sauropod remains in these rocks… somewhere!
Bottom: Gary Blackwell gets to work.

So how does a big lump of rock turn into a perfect looking fossil in the museum?

STAGE 1
Gary Blackwell, Dinosaur Isle's specimen specialist, shows me a big trolley holding chunks of grey rock. He shows me subtle changes in texture and colour that can only mean one thing: dinosaur bones. "Material arrives here in pieces of rock, from matchbox size, up to pieces you can barely lift", he says. "I assess each one, and form a plan of attack."

STAGE 2
Often the process starts by doing nothing at all to let the rock dry out. Then it gets brutal. For big chunks, Gary uses a grinder to make the first bold cuts… then one tool after another, each finer than the next one, to get closer and closer to the bone. "The smallest is a tiny vibrating point chisel that looks and sounds like a dentist's drill", he says. "It's so fine that I need to use a magnifying glass to see it!"

STAGE 3
Gary says: "I use a toothbrush for the most delicate cleaning. The toughest part is getting iron pyrite – fool's gold – off the surface of a bone. Sometimes I pick it off one crystal at a time."

STAGE 4
Fossils are polished with fine blasts of air. And baking soda is then used to remove any remaining dirt (yes, that's baking soda – also used to make gingerbread men!).

STAGE 5
Finally Gary protects the surface with an invisible coating… and hey presto! After months, if not years of work, there's a nice, clean bone, ready to go on display. "The satisfaction is huge," says Gary.

Dinosaur Isle Culver Parade, Sandown, Isle of Wight PO36 8QA
Tel: 01983 404344 dinosaurisle.com

MY EPIC ADVENTURE

Ace reporter **Diana Saw** went on a dino safari at Brook Chine, where entire skeletons have been found. Read all about her amazing adventures with dinosaur bones, squirting 'stones', and much, much more…

DIANA SAW'S SCOOP!

14:40 I arrive at Brook Chine car park, where I meet up with our guide Felicity 'Flick' Hawthorn (wearing a bright green coat) and 38 other hunters on a dinosaur safari.

15:00 The sun breaks through the clouds, as Flick answers the questions that we all want to ask. Yes, you can keep anything you find on the beach, so long as you can carry it… even if you find a dinosaur! However footcasts are protected, so you have to leave them on the beach.

15:07 Flick gets out a bag of rocks and we pass around sea sponge fossil, crystals, fossilised fish teeth and bones, fool's gold, fossilised wood and sea urchin fossils. Flick says that dinosaur hunters should look for shiny black stones with white speckles, honeycomb or even sparkly crystals inside. The crystals glint in the sunlight, which can make them easy to spot. The bone may have regular ridges or markings on the outside.

15:20 On the beach, Flick points out the banks and drifts of stones. We were told to look in the flint mounds for marine fossils and crystals, and go to the lower beach for dinosaur fossils. Then she turns us loose. We start prowling around, eyes to the ground.

BOOTIFUL

15:44 Luchen, 6, from London shows Flick another dinosaur bone fragment – it's small but perfectly marked.

15:45 A little girl with a big bag of fool's gold asks Flick how much more she needs to be rich. Unfortunately, it's not the right sort of gold to pay for mansions and limos… but it's very pretty.

15:49 We are half way around the bay. Flick rounds us up and gives a little talk on how dinosaurs came to be fossilised here. She points at the cliffs. Near the top, people have found Neolithic arrow heads, woolly mammoths, and fossilised deer. At the bottom, are the dinosaur remains.

15:58 We walk on towards Hanover Point. We see lots of iron pyrite (fool's gold) and bits of fossilised wood. Flick says this is a good sign, as these come from the same rocks as the dinosaur bones.

ISLE OF WIGHT Official Dinosaur Safari Guide

15:33 All the children are getting excited. Maddy, 8, from Worthing brings Flick some lovely golden pyrite crystals. Flick tells her how they form in the rock.

15:35 Sophia, 7, from London finds a flat rock with a brown blob on. Flick tells her it is a live sea anemone, not a fossil! Sophia pokes it and it squirts her. I'm not sure who is more surprised, Sophia or the anemone! Mum discourages her from taking it home, so it goes back in a rockpool.

15:36 Graham from Salisbury presents Flick with our first piece of dinosaur. It's a super specimen – a nice piece of leg bone. He shows us where he found it – exactly where Flick had told us to look. Flick calls everyone over to show them Graham's find.

15:59 Isabelle, 5, from Worthing finds a little piece of dinosaur bone.

16:08 Flick asks the 15 children to draw a dinosaur footprint. The beach is soon covered in three-toed feet. She explains how dinosaur footcasts were formed then leads us to them.

16:15 At Hanover Point, we gather round a beautiful footcast and chat about what life would have been like as a dinosaur. Flick tells us about Iguanodons. The first ever complete one was found here 100 years ago – it was sold for £20, and is in London's Natural History Museum. Now a single carnivore claw is valued at £7,000.

16:24 We look at a perfectly preserved small footcast with narrow toes. It's from a Hypsilophodon.

16:35 We head back along beach. I ask Flick about her own favourite finds. She says: "A dinosaur leg bone about 50 centimetres long, and three Iguanodon vertebrae that I found separately but which all fit together."

Dexter, 9, from the Isle of Wight is still going strong and gets the last find of the day - a piece of shale with a jumble of fossilised fish bones, spines and teeth.

17:00 Back at the car park, Flick says her goodbyes and does a brisk trade in shark teeth and other goodies. It's been a wonderful afternoon!

Thanks to **Island Gems Fossil and Dinosaur Walks.** Tel: 01983 740493, island-gems.co.uk
You can also book with...
Dinosaur Isle. Tel: 01983 404344, dinosaurisle.com
Dinosaur Expeditions. Tel: 01983 740844 or 07837 728810, dinosaurexpeditions.co.uk
Dr Steven Sweetman (specialist walks only). Tel: 07860 499851, email: s@mys.uk.com

IN THE FOOTSTEPS OF GIANTS

Do not, we repeat, *do not* miss seeing the amazing stone blocks containing real dinosaur footcasts on the beach at Hanover Point.

These casts were formed when heavy dinosaurs made footprints in soft mud. These footprints then filled with sand, which later turned to rock, keeping the shape of the footprints in the form of sandstone casts.

Some are huge, up to 70cm across. Most have three broad toes and probably belong to Iguanodon (see your spotter's guide on page 16). Smaller ones with narrow pointed toes are probably from flesh eating dinosaurs. Rarer types also turn up, with a rounder shape and more toes, probably from heavy Sauropods or Polacanthus.

As if that wasn't enough, at very low tides, dinosaur footprints are visible in the rock surface.

Close by, are sections of fossilised tree trunks up to a metre across. This is called the 'fossil forest' though in fact the trees are all fallen trunks of huge pine trees from the dinosaur times, dating back 125 million years.

Please…

- **Leave the footcasts where you find them** so other people can enjoy them. They belong to the National Trust and Crown Estates who own and care for this part of the beautiful coast.

- **Be careful of tide and sea conditions.** It's safest to go on a group walk with a guide.

ISLE OF WIGHT Official Dinosaur Safari Guide

GET ON THE GOOD FOOT!

Take a selfie or ask someone to take a picture of you standing on a dinosaur footcast. Stick it here, over this happy hunter.

Also tweet your pics to @visitIOW – we'd love to see them. Use #dinoselfie

STICK YOUR PHOTO HERE

Compton Bay is among the **'TOP 50 BEST BEACHES IN THE WORLD'** – Sunday Times Travel Magazine

GETTING HERE

Hanover Point, in Compton Bay, is midway along the beach between Shippards Chine and Brook Chine. National Trust members can park for free.

SPOTTER'S GUIDE

Over 20 different types of dinosaur have been found on the Island, making this one of the best places in the world for the dinosaur hunter. The first specimens were discovered in the 1820s and new varieties are still being unearthed today, sometimes by children just digging around on the beach. Bones, teeth and entire skeletons have been discovered around the Island. So next time you're on one of the Island's beaches, make sure you're on full alert for the following fossilised beasts...

KEY

MEAT EATER:

PLANT EATER:

FISH EATER:

ROAR RATING:
This is our guide to how scary it would be to meet one of these beasts on a dark and stormy night. One symbol means 'Ooh that's a bit scary' – five symbols means 'RUN FOR IT!!!'

IGUANODON

This was the first ever dinosaur to be found on the Island. Experts think that it roamed in herds, rather like the wildebeests in Africa today. It had distinctive large thumb spikes and a beak.

DIET:

LENGTH: 9 metres

ROAR RATING:

LOOK FOR ME: From Compton Bay to Atherfield Point; and Yaverland

POLACANTHUS FOXII

This was a huge spiky creature from the Ankylosaur family, with spines and armour on its back. Its name means 'many thorns' and the foxii is a reference to Rev Fox (see page 26) who first discovered this dino on the Island in 1865. Not much is known about this dinosaur as there are not many fossil remains... so watch out for this one!

DIET:

LENGTH: 4-5 metres

ROAR RATING:

LOOK FOR ME: Around Brighstone Bay

PTEROSAUR

These flying lizards flapped and glided through the sky. Some were as big as hang-gliders, others as small as crows. Their long toothed beaks were used to catch fish with a big gulp! Species include Caulkicephalus and Daisy Morris's Vectidraco. By Early Cretaceous times they shared the skies with the earliest birds.

DIET:

LENGTH: 4-5 metres

ROAR RATING:

LOOK FOR ME: Sandown Bay, Atherfield, Compton Bay

YIKES!

If you looked up in dinosaur times, you would have seen terrifying flying lizards. In the water, you'd find crocodiles, turtles, sharks and armoured fish – and fossils of all these have been found around the Island's coast.

ISLE OF WIGHT Official Dinosaur Safari Guide

SHARP!

Finger bones from a small carnivorous dinosaur called Eotyrannus lengi on display at Dinosaur Isle, Sandown

VALDOSAURUS

EOTYRANNUS

DANGER!

NEOVENATOR

DANGER!

Meet this light, fast little fellow – he grazed on leaves rather like a gazelle today. This species was first discovered on the Island.

DIET: 🍃
LENGTH: 4-5 metres
ROAR RATING: 📢📢
LOOK FOR ME: Around Brighstone Bay and anywhere else on the South West coast

The world's first specimen of Eotyrannus, an early relative of Tyrannosaurus rex, was also found on the Island. It had powerful hind legs and very long fingers. Eotyrannus lengi was named after local collector Gavin Leng (see page 27).

DIET: 🥩
LENGTH: 4-5 metres
ROAR RATING: 📢📢📢
LOOK FOR ME: Around Brighstone Bay on the South West of the Island

This was one of the largest and most ferocious predators. The world's best specimen was found by a family holidaying on the Isle of Wight, in the summer of 1978.

DIET: 🥩
LENGTH: 7.5 metres
ROAR RATING: 📢📢📢📢📢
LOOK FOR ME: Around Brighstone Bay on the South West of the Island

HYPSILOPHODON

SAUROPOD

BARYONYX

These were small two-legged creatures, with teeth and a beak, and they were probably very fast runners. However they couldn't run fast enough to escape what experts think was a flash-flood, as a whole herd of them was found buried on the Island. This is the only place they've ever been found.

DIET: 🍃
LENGTH: 1-3 metres
ROAR RATING: 📢📢
LOOK FOR ME: Brighstone Bay

These giants had a long neck for reaching leaves, chisel-shaped teeth for cropping vegetation, a vast stomach for digestion, a long tail, and broad legs to support their enormous weight.

DIET: 🍃
LENGTH: 15-20 metres
ROAR RATING: 📢📢📢
LOOK FOR ME: Brighstone Bay, between Chilton Chine and Sudmoor Point

Another special find has been the huge Baryonyx, whose long claws and a narrow jaw suggest that it may have evolved to catch and eat fish from the rivers and lagoons.

DIET:
LENGTH: 10 metres
ROAR RATING:
LOOK FOR ME: Anywhere on the South West of the Island

Steve says Don't go digging around in cliffs – it's too dangerous. See what you can find on the beach!

YAVERLAND SAFARI

Look for black layers in the exposed rock – these are the dinosaur beds.

Steve says I like this walk because you can explore 30 million years in a mile. Plus it's along a glorious sandy beach and right by a carpark with ice creams and toilets. This is the most accessible beach for people with limited mobility or small children.

Start at the Dinosaur Meteorite in Yaverland car park.

DISTANCE: CLIFF TOP SECTION: 3 MILES | BEACH SECTION: UP TO 2 MILES

CLIFF WALK

1 Follow the sign-posted Coastal Path until you reach the top of the landslip. You'll get views over some of the richest dinosaur beds on the Island.

2 Continue to the top of Culver Down. You are now right on top of the huge slab of chalk that used to lie on top of the dinosaur beds and now forms a ridge that runs across the Island to the Needles in the West. Check out the amazing views across Sandown Bay.

3 Go back the way you came. See how the cliff line changes in colour (from grey and brown to orange, grey and white) as the environment changed from land to sea before the rocks were tilted on edge. The rocks date from the Cretaceous period, between 66 and 145 million years ago, when dinosaurs were King.

BEACH WALK

1 Stroll along the beach with the sea on your right. The landslip here has washed down many dinosaur fossils onto the beach. Look for large pieces of flat rock – these are packed with small fossilised oyster shells and may also contain fish bones, scales and teeth. Walk as far as you like – but for your own safety, please watch out for the tide, stay away from the cliff and don't climb up the landslip.

2 Turn around and retrace your steps, back along the beach to the car park.

YAVERLAND SAFARI FIND LOG:

DATE OF SAFARI:

LOCATION:
DESCRIPTION:

LOCATION:
DESCRIPTION:

LOCATION:
DESCRIPTION:

Scales from the armoured Polacanthus have been found at Yaverland.

FOX SAFARI

ISLE OF WIGHT Official Dinosaur Safari Guide

Steve says Rev Fox was a pioneer whom I picture on a sunny day, weighing up whether to do the parish rounds or go off fossil hunting. It seems the fossils generally won! This walk goes from his home to the dinosaur beds – he must have walked it hundreds of times.

Follow in the footsteps of Victorian dinosaur hunter Rev William Fox. Start at the public car park in Brighstone (behind the Three Bishops pub on Main Road).

DISTANCE: 4 MILES

FOX SAFARI FIND LOG:

DATE OF SAFARI:

LOCATION:
DESCRIPTION:

LOCATION:
DESCRIPTION:

LOCATION:
DESCRIPTION:

1. Walk up to Main Road, cross, and go down North Street past the thatched library and museum.

2. Myrtle Cottage, home of Reverend Fox, is marked by a green plaque. Return to Main Road and turn right (West) to follow the road for a mile.

3. Turn left onto Chilton Lane and follow it for a mile. You will pass Chilton Farm on your left.

4. The road turns sharp right, but go straight ahead and follow the footpath signs. Take the footpath signposted BS71 and follow this to the Military Road / A3055. Cross and continue straight ahead to the beach.

5. Walk along the beach with the sea to your right. The cliffs here contain all the classic dinosaur bed features – red and grey clays and darker debris beds, all constantly eroding and releasing the fresh material that Reverend Fox would have been collecting. See pages 8-9 for what to look for.

6. Stop at Grange Chine - the carnivore Neovenator was found near here by holiday visitors. Take the track back up the cliff, through the holiday site to the Military Road.

7. Cross the road and follow the paths signed for Brighstone back to the village centre. Back in Brighstone, there's St Mary's churchyard where inscriptions on some of the gravestones show how perilous the sea was to a fishing community. You could also visit the Seven coffee house which is a Tourist Information Point and where you can book guided dinosaur walks.

You're in dinosaur country – the red and grey clay and darker debris beds are the giveaway.

DINOSAUR ISLAND

Red Funnel Red Jet
Southampton – West Cowe

WEST COWES

Wightlink car ferry
Yarmouth – Lymington

YARMOUTH

REFLECTIONS FOSSIL SHOP

FRESHWATER

NEEDLES SAFARI

FOOTPRINT SAFARI

• COMPTON METEORITE

NEEDLES VIEWPOINT METEORITE

Iguanodon
Sauropod
Aristosuchus
Pterosaur • Hanover Point
Sauropod
Pterosaur
Eucamerutus
Iguanodon

BRIGHSTONE FOX SAFARI

FOSSIL HOT SPOT

DINOSAUR EXPEDITION CENTRE

FOSSIL HOT SPOT

COMPTON BAY

Polacanthus
Iguanodon
Eotyrannus
Neovenator
Aristosuchus
Baryonyx
Hypsilophodus
Valdosaurus
Vectidraco
Iguanodon
• Atherfiel

BRIGHSTONE BAY

DINOSAUR ISLAND · THE OFFICIAL DINOSAUR CAPITAL OF THE UK · DINOSAUR ISLAND

EXPLORERS' MAP

Red Funnel car ferry
Southampton – East Cowes

EAST COWES

Wightlink car ferry
Portsmouth – Fishbourne

Wightlink catamaran
Portsmouth Harbour – Ryde Pier

FISHBOURNE

RYDE

Hovertravel hovercraft
Southsea – Ryde

NEWPORT

BEMBRIDGE

YAVERLAND SAFARI
YAVERLAND METEORITE
• Yaverlandia
Polacanthus
Caulkicephalus
Iguanodon
Baryonyx
DINOSAUR ISLE Sauropod

FOSSIL HOT SPOT

SANDOWN BAY

GODSHILL
ISLAND GEMS
FOSSIL SHOP & WALKS

SHANKLIN
JURASSIC JIM
FOSSIL SHOP
FOSSIL CAVERN

VENTNOR
Ventnor Botanic Garden
• **BONCHURCH METEORITE**
• **VENTNOR METEORITE**

ALE
• BLACKGANG CHINE
• **BLACKGANG VIEWPOINT METEORITE**

THE FOOTPRINT SAFARI

You can see footcasts poking out of the sand

Steve says I like this walk because the Hanover Point footcasts are the most spectacular evidence of prehistoric life that you'll find anywhere in Britain – and you can see them right there on the beach!

Start at Shippards Chine car park.

LONG ROUTE: 4 MILES | SHORT ROUTE: 2 MILES

1 Check out the Meteorite starring the virtual Iguanodon (see page 29).

2 Follow the signposted Coastal Path, walking with the sea to your left.

3 At the signpost "Public Footpath F68 to Beach" go down the staircase to the beach.

4 Follow the shore with the sea to your right. This is Compton Bay, site of many amazing finds including part of a large Sauropod. Constant erosion of the landslip makes this one of the best stretches on the Island for fossil hunting. The finds are washed onto the beach, so don't go near the cliffs – they're dangerous and you don't need to!

5 You'll see the car park where you started up on your left. Let's just say that it's smaller than it used to be, thanks to coastal erosion, and there used to be beach huts here too. Walk on, with the sea to your right. At low tide, you can seen the remains of a shipwrecked steam tug – bones from an armoured Polacanthus were discovered nearby.

6 Carry on to the bit of land that juts out – this is Hanover Point, the best place in Britain to see dinosaur footcasts (see pages 14-15). At very low tides you can also get out to see dinosaur tracks and the 'fossil forest' of petrified tree trunks. It's safest to go on a tour.

7 Look around you at the spectacular landslip… which just keeps on slipping.

8 Carry on to Brook Bay, where you can forage for fossils among the flints.

9 When you get to Brook Chine, take the gravel track up to the car park. Take the signposted coastal route and walk with the sea to your left. You'll get amazing views of the red and grey dinosaur beds and the chalk that was once on top of them. Return to where you started, at Shippards Chine car park.

Short route: From Shippards Chine car park, go down to the steps to the beach, turn left… and start walking. Follow the steps above (from No 5).

FOOTPRINT SAFARI FIND LOG:

DATE OF SAFARI:

LOCATION:

DESCRIPTION:

LOCATION:

DESCRIPTION:

LOCATION:

DESCRIPTION:

Footprint trail exposed at low tide at Hanover Point.

THE NEEDLES SAFARI

ISLE OF WIGHT Official Dinosaur Safari Guide

ALUM BAY
THE NEEDLES
THE NEEDLES OLD BATTERY
SCRATCHELL'S BAY
THE NEEDLES LANDMARK ATTRACTION

Steve says This walk takes you right to the end of the dinosaurs – and the end of the Island. The poet Sir John Betjeman once said that, "One feels that Western Wight is an earthquake poised in mid explosion". Stand at the Needles viewpoint and you'll see what he meant.

Start at the car park for The Needles Landmark Attraction.

CLIFF TOP WALK: 3 MILES | BEACH WALK: 2 MILES

BEACH WALK

1 Head into The Needles Landmark Attraction. Follow the marked path down to Alum Bay (it's tucked away, to the left of the chairlift). Alternatively take the chairlift down – it's great fun.

2 Walk along the beach, with the sea to your right. Admire the famous Alum Bay coloured sands (pictured), which form the cliffs here. They were laid down around 50 million years ago and there are 21 recognised colours. You can't dig them up – but back at the Park, you can create your own souvenir by layering the pretty sands into a shaped bottle.

3 If you go right into the corner of Alum Bay, you'll come face-to-face with the wall of chalk. This used to be the top of the chalk bed before it tilted by 90 degrees in a great geological heave-ho. The layer of chalk was formed just before the dinosaurs were wiped out at the end of the Cretaceous era. That makes this little corner as close as you can get to the very end of the dinosaur age. Yes, this is sad, but it's probably just as well – doubt dinos would make very good pets!

CLIFF WALK

1 Take the road signposted to the Old Battery that leads you up the side of the Down (or catch the Needles Breezer bus).

2 As you go up, you'll have magnificent views over Alum Bay.

3 You'll pass the Old Battery, which was built in the Victorian times to guard the Island, and later used for rocket testing.

4 Carry on to the New Battery at the top, which was manned during both World Wars. The Dinosaur Meteorite here stars the giant plant eater, Pelorosaurus.

5 Follow the signed footpath to the Needles Viewpoint. This is the best view you'll get of the Needles. You're now standing on a wall of chalk, up to half a mile high, that buried many dinosaurs.

6 Retrace your steps to the Needles Park.

NEEDLES SAFARI FIND LOG:

DATE OF SAFARI:

LOCATION:
DESCRIPTION:

LOCATION:
DESCRIPTION:

LOCATION:
DESCRIPTION:

DINOSAUR PLANT SAFARI

Conifers

Ferns

Dinosaurs on the Isle of Wight didn't eat grass.... because grass didn't exist back then. That came millions of years later. In fact flowers didn't exist then either.

Instead, the ground was covered with:

 Ferns - like the giant ferns we have today.

 Conifers - cone bearing trees like pines.

 Cycads - which are seed plants with a thick, woody trunk and stiff evergreen leaves. They look a bit like pineapples.

We know this because fossils of these plants have been found in the Island's dinosaur beds (see Freaky Fact), and they often wash out onto the beaches. The treasures found by hunters just like you include fossil leaves, pine cones, entire tree trunks and even charcoal from prehistoric forest fires.

At Ventnor Botanic Garden, close to where the Valdosaurus would have enjoyed many vegetarian meals, you can see the modern relatives of the prehistoric plants (botanic.co.uk). Examples include the Monkey Puzzle Tree, Modern Gymnosperms, Ginkgo Tree and Tree Ferns.

If you're going in the summer, look out for the little green Ventnor lizards, scuttling around between the rocks in the terraces and basking in the sun. They're not dinosaurs… but use your imagination, and they just might be.

DINNER TIME

They might look big and scary – but many of the dinosaurs were softies at heart and preferred eating plants to other creatures. For example, a typical meal for Ventnor's Valdosaurus might be as follows…

Dino's dinner menu

Starter of lush green ferns, freshly foraged from the forest

Main course of organic conifer leaves topped with locally sourced pine cones

Amuse-bouche of a little stone or two

Dessert of the finest cycads with a smattering of small twigs

PREHISTORIC JOKE

Q. How did Neovenator like his steaks?
A. ROAAAAAR!!

Some dinosaurs, such as Neovenator and Eotyrannus, were carnivores and ate meat.

ISLE OF WIGHT Official Dinosaur Safari Guide

✓ Cycads

✗ No flowers, fruit or grass

So you want proof that there were plants?

Traces of plant roots from when this rock was in the soil 130m years ago.

Cretaceous pine cones found on the Isle of Wight.

Sections of a pine tree trunk from the fossilised forest at Hanover Point.

Bed of densely packed plant debris from the Early Cretaceous at Yaverland.

Fossilised wood encrusted with sea-worn iron pyrite (fool's gold).

A large chunk of fossilised wood, on the beach at Compton (plus Toby).

MEET THE RELATIVES

Which of these creatures are the closest relatives of the dinosaurs?
1. Birds   2. Lizards.   3. Frogs.

Answer – birds. Some experts say that they actually are dinosaurs. Birds are thought to have evolved from small dinosaurs called theropods (whose name means 'beast feet') up to 145 million years ago.

FREAKY FACT

A dinosaur bed is a layer of rock where dinosaur remains can be found… it's nothing to do with where they used to sleep!

FAMOUS FOSSIL HUNTERS

These epic adventurers left no stone unturned when it came to finding fantastic fossils on the Isle of Wight…

DADDY DINO

The **Reverend William D. Fox** (1813-1881) was the Island's earliest known dinosaur hunter. He was a curate at the church in Brighstone, although it was said that it was "always bones first and the parish next". He found over 500 specimens including completely new dinosaurs, four of which have been named after him. His collection is now in the Natural History Museum.

DINO DETECTIVE

Nick Chase is one of the Island's most successful dinosaur hunters – he's out most days, searching for his next big find. With amazing beginner's luck, his very first discovery was an Iguanodon skull on a camping trip. "We then found more of it too. It is now in the Natural History Museum."

And his favourite fossils? "The Iguanodon, of course! And the Valdosaurus that's on display at Dinosaur Isle. Plus a crocodile, shark, and now another near-complete Iguanodon."

Nick is pictured above with some of his treasures. The big fossils by his knees are the thigh bones of an Iguanodon. Many of the other bones are pieces of a giant Sauropod. Nick stores these in his study (which doubles as his kitchen) until he can donate them to museums.

DAISY DINO

Daisy Morris is a fossil hunter, the Children's Ambassador for Visit Isle of Wight, and a schoolgirl who lives on the Island.

When she was just four she found a fossil at Atherfield beach. "I showed it to a local fossil expert who then took it to Southampton University for more experts to look at it," she recalls.

"The fossil took a long time to be checked and identified but in 2013 when I was 9 it was officially named and released as a new species, 'Vectidraco daisymorrisae' (the first part means Isle of Wight Dragon, the species part is named after me!)."

Daisy donated it to The Natural History Museum in London in 2011. She says proudly: "My fossil now shares a drawer with some of Mary Anning's pterosaur fossils – she was a famous fossil hunter in Victorian times."

Can you guess what this fossil is? It's probably from a dinosaur.
A: Intestine. B: Dung. C: Toe.

Answer: It's B, dino dung, also known as coprolite! This prehistoric plop was dumped by a dinosaur (or another big beast) 130 million years ago. Similar lumps have been found on the Island's beaches.

Nick Chase's expert advice:
"When you are walking along the beach, don't look hard for something that resembles a dinosaur or a bone. Relax your eyes and scan for pieces that just look a bit different to the other stones."

ISLE OF WIGHT Official Dinosaur Safari Guide

 **One bored dad got fed up with fossil hunting and fell asleep on the beach – he woke up to find that the annoying stone digging into his back was in fact an Iguanodon bone!**

Photo: Max Wooldridge

DR DINO

While most people hunt for big dinosaurs, Islander **Dr Steve Sweetman** seeks out the little ones. The palaeontologist crushes and filters buckets of rock from the dinosaur beds to find bones and teeth from the many small animals that lived among the giants. He has already found more than 50 new species.

His first exciting discovery came at the age of four, when he found "a fossilised sea urchin on the beach at Cowes". Then as a teenager, he made another find on the Island's south west coast: "a carnivore tooth from a relative of Velociraptor."

His personal favourite is not a dinosaur, but "a newt-like creature called Wesserpeton that's new to science. It is the smallest four-legged creature from dinosaur times ever found in the world."

Dr Sweetman's advice to someone just starting is: "Go on a guided walk. And if you do find something important, donate it to a museum - then your name will be attached to it forever."

DINO MIGHT

In 1992, amateur fossil hunter **Gavin Leng** found a neck bone from a giant Sauropod between Clinton Chine and Sudmoor Point. The beast was thought to have been more than 20m long - that's the length of two double decker buses. Five years later, he found a dinosaur claw from a new, scary species – it was named Eotyrannus lengi after him ('Leng's early tyrant'). You can see a model at Dinosaur Isle, and parts of the skull and hand.

WANT TO BE FAMOUS?

Hunters on the Isle of Wight have found fossils of nearly all the main groups of dinosaurs, including no fewer than four big carnivore species. But no-one has yet found a dinosaur egg, even though between them the Island's dinosaurs must have laid millions. Nobody's found a dinosaur feather here either (they've been discovered in China). We're also still looking for a Polacanthus skull – this would be the first in the world.
So fame (and possibly fortune) await whoever is the first to make any of these finds…

DINO MORE

Martin Simpson has spent over 35 years finding fossils on the Island. He had 68,000 fossils at the last count – and at least 60 new species including fossilised lobsters, ammonites, crocodiles, and also dinosaur-age insects preserved in amber. His advice to beginners is: "As soon as you can, concentrate on getting to know one type of fossil or one collecting place really well, as this will improve your chances of finding something really special".

STICK YOUR PHOTO HERE

Name:

MEET THE VIRTUAL DINOSAURS

Who wants to meet a dinosaur? You do? Well… sorry. You're 115 million years too late. However you can encounter the next best thing – a real, live virtual dinosaur!

Visit Isle of Wight, the official Tourist Board for the Island, has created an epic App for dinosaur hunters, and it's totally FREE. The App will take you on a trail of discovery around the Island's dinosaur coast, using augmented reality technology. There are six 'Dinosaur Meteors' along the way and when you hook up to them with your smart phone, you'll be able to see full sized dinosaurs moving around, just where the real ones used to roam. Have fun and take a snap or make a video, starring you and your prehistoric pal. Tweet pics to us @visitIOW using #dinoselfie

GET THE DINO APP

Android users: Go to Google Play Store and search for 'Dinosaur Island Isle of Wight'. Click on the 'install' button to upload the app.

iPhone and iPad users: Go to the iTunes store and search for 'Dinosaur Island Isle of Wight' then click 'install' to upload the app.

Go to visitisleofwight.co.uk/dinosaur-island for the lowdown including the exact locations of the meteors.

STICK YOUR DINO ENCOUNTER PHOTO HERE

ISLE OF WIGHT Official Dinosaur Safari Guide

THE BEASTS YOU'LL MEET ON YOUR JOURNEY AROUND THE ISLAND

METEOR 1: YAVERLAND

Iguanodon – these were big, mean… vegetarians! They had scary thumb spikes, which would have been good for fighting and foraging.

METEOR 2: BONCHURCH

Polacanthus – the name means 'many thorns', as they were spiky and covered in armour. This made them good warriors – and also stopped bigger predators from snacking on them!

METEOR 3: VENTNOR

Valdosaurus – this was a two-legged little plant-eater that skipped around on two legs. They were fast, and when under attack had one simple strategy: run for it!!

METEOR 4: BLACKGANG VIEWPOINT

Caulkicephalus – this flying reptile had an amazing wingspan and lots of teeth. This killer combination enabled them to catch fish while on the move.

METEOR 5: COMPTON

Neovenator – this brute was a carnivore and one of the top predators of its day. They were fast, fierce… and showed no mercy.

METEOR 6: NEEDLES VIEWPOINT

Pelorosaurus – a mighty giant whose name means 'monstrous lizard', but in fact you had little to fear unless you were a plant (they were veggie). You'd be in trouble if one sat on you though, as they grew to 20m.

TIME TRAVEL

The dinosaur themed Island Coaster bus will take you to each meteor. Or cycle – this is Bicycle Island as well as Dinosaur Island!

AMAZING ANIMATRONICS

See roaring, stomping dinosaurs at Blackgang Chine.

DINODRAW

DIANA SAW'S SCOOP!

Want to know more about the secret life of a famous dinosaur artist? Our roving reporter Diana Saw did – so she stopped by John Sibbick's office to watch the illustrator at work….

When he was a boy, on holiday in Shanklin, John Sibbick started drawing dinosaurs... and basically hasn't stopped! He now lives in Shanklin, and has illustrated so many books that there's no room for them all in his house. You can see his work in Dinosaur Isle and many other museums - and maybe even on your own doormat, as he's designed stamps for the Royal Mail.

John uses special Gouache paints for their strong, powerful colours. He has very fine brushes and coloured pencils to pick out the important details, such as terrible claws, snapping jaws and angry eyes.

He's famous for his detailed landscapes, which take a lot of research. Says John: "I study the fossil record to make sure that every plant is correct for the time I am illustrating. Over the course of the dinosaur age, plants evolved from ferns, horsetails and cycads, to flowering plants and grasses. To get the dinosaur plants just right, I go to see some of them at Ventnor Botanic Garden."

His favourite dinosaurs to draw are the 'duck-billed dinosaurs', including the Island's Iguanodons. Says John: "We can picture how they lived in herds, migrating and feeding with their young alongside."

For more information about John's amazing work, visit johnsibbick.com

ISLE OF WIGHT Official Dinosaur Safari Guide

SO HOW DO WE KNOW WHAT COLOUR DINOS WERE?

The answer is: we don't. Dinosaurs could have been pink, purple, spotted, striped, they might even have glowed in the dark… nobody knows for sure. "Until someone finds fossilised pigments, it has to be intelligent guesswork", says artist John Sibbick.

He tends to go for army-style browns and green, with pops of eye-catching colours, like orange or blue. "That's because just like modern animals, they needed neutral colours and disruptive patterns for camouflage, but also flashes of bright colour for recognition and to attract mates," he explains.

DINO COLOUR SWATCH

| BAD BOY BLUE | STINKY SLIME GREEN | SHOW-OFF PINK | BLOOD & GUTS RED |

 DRAW-A-SAURUS

Design your own dino in this space - and don't forget to name it after yourself!

John Sibbick says: "Look at models, skeletons, books, museums and modern animals. Get a feel for how skeletons and muscles fit together to give shape and movement to your dinosaurs."

31

EPIC ACTIVITIES... EPIC ACTIVITIES... EPIC ACTIVITIES... EPIC ACTIVITIES

ARE YOU A GEEKOSAURUS?

How well do you know your dinosaurs? Find out over the next four pages. There's a quiz below, plus spot the difference and a giant wordsearch to puzzle over. You will get points for each one. Check out your score on page 35.

1 The Iguanodon trampled all over Compton, leaving footprints behind. How many toes did this dinosaur have?

a. 2   b. 3   c. 17

2 Let's go back to the Cretaceous times, between 66 and 145 million years ago. The area that's now the Isle of Wight was:

a. Hot dry land.
b. Swamped by warm wet lagoons.
c. Under the sea.

3 Experts found bones from a herd of Hypsilophodon dinosaurs, huddled together, on the south of the Island. There were at least 20 of them. How do you think they met their end?

a. A forest fire.
b. A flood.
c. They ate each other.

4 How many types of dinosaur were named after the Victorian collector Reverend Fox?

a. 1   b. 4   c. 16

5 In 1995, dinosaur hunter Gavin Leng found a new type of dinosaur that's has been named after him. Was it…

a. Gavinus gavini.
b. Eotyrannus lengi.
c. Tyrannosaurus gavin.

6 The best places to go dinosaur hunting is:

a. On the beaches.
b. Up the cliffs.
c. In ploughed-up fields.

7 What haven't we found yet on the Isle of Wight?

a. Dinosaur eggs.
b. Dinosaur teeth.
c. Dinosaur claws.

8 Many dinosaur bones are black. This is because they…

a. Are covered in fossilised seaweed.
b. Have absorbed minerals from the water in the ground, which changes their colour.
c. Have been burnt by the hot sun.

9 How do dinosaur bones end up on Isle of Wight beaches?

a. They fall into the sea from the cliffs, and then get washed up on the beach.
b. Surfers see them floating on the sea and bring them onto the land.
c. Giant dolphins bring them over from Africa and burp them up on the beaches.

10 The diet of plant-eating dinosaurs included:

a. Ferns.   b. Grass.   c. Ice cream.

11 At Blackgang, you can watch a virtual Caulkicephalus fly around in the sky, thanks to the amazing Dinosaur Island App. The name Caulkicephalus makes a cheeky reference to…

a. 'Caulkheads' - people on the Isle of Wight who've lived here for a very long time.
b. 'Chalk heads' - teachers who prefer using blackboards to whiteboards.
c. 'Corgi heads' – dog lovers.

12 What is a cycad?

a. A huge insect with fangs.
b. A dinosaur dropping.
c. A pineapple-like plant.

13 Dinosaur bones are often found along with…

a. Fossilised wood.
b. Flint arrow heads.
c. Woolly mammoth bones.

14 Why do you think the Baryonyx dinosaurs had big jaws and sharp teeth, like a crocodile?

a. To catch fish, their favourite food.
b. To deter predators.
c. To stop cavemen attacking them.

15 Small, highly polished stones have been found in dinosaurs' stomachs. Why were they there?

a. They would rattle when the dinosaurs roared, to scare away predators.
b. The dinosaurs ate them – maybe they thought they looked tasty. Once they were in the stomach, they were used to grind food.
c. They were used as part of a weight loss programme.

16 This Isle of Wight dinosaur was a prickly customer with spiky armour. His name means 'many thorns'. Which dino are we talking about?

a. Stegosaurus.
b. Triceratops.
c. Polacanthus.

ISLE OF WIGHT Official Dinosaur Safari Guide

EPIC ACTIVITIES... EPIC ACTIVITIES... EPIC ACTIVITIES... EPIC ACTIVITIES...

SPOT THE DINO DIFFERENCES

TRAIN YOUR BRAIN

You need sharp eyes to find fossils on the beach so here's your chance to see if you've got what it takes to spot something unusual. There are six differences between these pictures of a mother and baby dinosaur. The picture on the left is just the way that the artist, John Sibbick, drew it. The picture on the right has had features added or removed. Can you spot the differences?

Scoring:
Give yourself 1 point for each difference you spot.

EPIC ACTIVITIES... EPIC ACTIVITIES... EPIC ACTIVITIES... EPIC ACTIVITIES

WICKED WORDSEARCH

D	T	T	E	S	C	A	R	N	I	V	O	R	E	B	I	X	X	Z	M
O	C	P	Q	L	F	O	S	S	I	L	V	F	N	I	B	C	A	H	D
O	B	O	I	W	I	B	O	J	W	Y	A	V	E	R	L	A	N	D	I
M	A	T	M	S	S	Z	A	W	U	J	N	T	O	G	T	W	H	R	N
E	R	H	U	P	L	J	L	E	W	I	F	I	V	L	G	K	A	D	O
T	Y	A	Y	U	T	E	H	S	G	B	O	N	E	J	X	F	J	U	S
E	O	N	S	P	L	O	O	P	I	Z	R	E	N	T	A	L	V	U	A
O	N	O	J	I	S	E	N	F	F	B	T	I	A	S	M	S	E	U	U
R	Y	V	C	C	S	I	P	I	W	I	U	Q	T	M	F	V	C	S	R
I	X	E	H	O	X	A	L	O	N	I	U	M	O	C	E	A	T	I	C
T	T	R	A	P	A	K	U	O	L	W	G	T	R	S	A	L	I	C	R
E	U	P	L	R	D	T	M	R	P	A	Z	H	O	T	T	D	D	L	O
N	R	O	K	O	O	M	E	Z	O	H	C	U	T	A	H	O	R	A	C
M	T	I	V	L	A	W	W	E	S	P	O	A	P	Y	E	S	A	W	O
A	L	N	M	I	K	Y	S	R	T	M	O	D	N	A	R	A	C	T	D
M	E	T	D	T	C	T	Z	H	X	H	I	D	O	T	A	U	O	O	I
R	T	P	N	E	Z	I	G	U	A	N	O	D	O	N	H	R	D	X	L
F	J	T	Q	M	S	E	W	R	L	R	W	C	Q	F	C	U	A	Q	E
K	D	M	T	S	W	P	R	W	A	Y	K	Z	C	P	O	S	S	A	X
E	O	T	Y	R	A	N	N	U	S	U	F	O	O	T	C	A	S	T	S

Time how long it takes you to find these hidden words:
SAFARI • ISLE OF WIGHT • DINOSAUR • CHALK • FOSSIL • AMMONITE • COPROLITE • BONE • FOOTCASTS
HANOVER POINT • IGUANODON • VALDOSAURUS • EOTYRANNUS • NEOVENATOR • POLACANTHUS
HYPSILOPHODON • SAUROPOD • BARYONYX • CARNIVORE • VECTIDRACO • CROCODILE • TURTLE
YAVERLAND • SHARK • TEETH • METEORITE • COMPTON • CLAW • EGG • FEATHER

Scoring:
Less that 5 minutes = 5 points. 5-10 minutes = 3 points. Over 10 minutes = 2 point.

EPIC ACTIVITIES... EPIC ACTIVITIES... EPIC ACTIVITIES... EPIC ACTIVITIES...

ANSWERS

TOP TIP: Stand on your head, or just turn the book upside down to read the answers!

1b. You can see their distinctive three toed footcasts all over the beach and footprints in the mud off Hanover Point. Iguanodons were vegetarian and had rounded toes – pointed toes are usually a sign of a meat-eating carnivore.

2. You'll get a point for any of these answers – as the land went through all of these stages in turn.

3b. Most dinosaurs from the Isle of Wight have been found in layers of mud, which suggests that they were caught up in a flood.

4b. This is still a world record.

5b. This was thought to be an early relative of Tyrannosaurus rex. You can see parts of the skull and hand, and a life sized model at Dinosaur Isle.

6a. The beaches are the only safe place, so long as you check the weather and tides. You can keep what you pick up, so long as it's not a footcast or footprint. Everywhere else is unsafe... and illegal.

7a. We've found lots of claws and teeth... now all we need are some lovely dinosaur eggs. They must be out there somewhere, so get hunting!

8b. During the fossilisation process, the bone is replaced by iron minerals, changing the colour from white to black. This also makes them heavy, so sometimes they sink into the sand and you can only see the tip.

9a. The cliffs are the source of all of our amazing fossils. Many of them are smoothed by the waves and end up as pebbles. Others keep their shape and textures.

10a. Ferns were a tasty treat. Grass and ice cream didn't exist back then!

11a. To be a Cauldhead, you need to be able to date both sides of your family back by at least two generations!

12c. Cycad plants go back to dinosaur times. You can see their fossils at Dinosaur Isle and living specimens at Ventnor Botanic Garden.

13a. Dinosaurs and trees often got buried together in layers of mud, following a flood. So if you find fossilised wood, then keep looking for bones – as you're on the right track. Flint arrow heads and mammoth bones have been found on the island but are more recent than the dinosaurs.

14. Get a point for a or b. Cavemen came millions of years later!

15d. These stomach stones, known as 'gastroliths', helped their digestion. Many birds today (including chickens and ostriches) swallow pebbles and grit for the same reason.

16c. Polacanthus – the scales, known as 'scutes', are up to 30cm across (the size of your ruler!).

HOW DID YOU DO?

18 and above: Are you *actually* a dinosaur? You certainly know a lot about them! Congratulations, geekosaurus!

10-17: You're good. Very good. Time to start thinking about writing your own book now?

0-9: Don't worry about it. Some people are better at finding fossils than answering quizzes! Read some more of this book, then take the tests again. Good luck!

SPECIMENS:
George (age 10 years) + Woolly Mammoth leg bone (age 10,000 years)

ON THE TRAIL OF JURASSIC JIM

DIANA SAW'S SCOOP!

Our star reporter, **Diana Saw**, gives us the lowdown on **Jurassic Jim**, a shop filled with dinosaur fossils, minerals and curious things to make your eyes pop out of your head…

FREAKY FINDS
1. WOOLLY MAMMOTH HAIR
2. MOSASAUR (PREDATOR X) TEETH
3. FOSSILISED SHARK POO

All available at Jurassic Jim's.

Tucked between teashops in the pretty town of Shanklin is something strange. Something extraordinary. Something… well, you get the picture. We're talking about Jurassic Jim: a fossil emporium like no other. It's staffed by working palaeontologists, who hunt and gather up to 80% of the stock in the shop – and also supply museums and wholesalers with their amazing finds.

"We go all over the world to find fossils – and spend lots of time on the Island's beaches too", says owner 'Jurassic' Jim, who started collecting fossils when he was an eight year old boy. "On the Island, my favourite place is Yaverland, as you can pick up the most diverse range of fossils."

Every surface, every corner, is packed with fossils and gemstones, and any space left is filled with African art. The stock changes all the time, according to whatever Jim and his team have found. You might discover monster sharks' teeth, fossilised fish, pumice stone from a real volcano, mammoth hair, bug necklaces, gemstone skulls, dinosaur stomach stones, or even polished Jurassic shark poo.

Unlike most shops, kids are encouraged to touch, as Jim's philosophy is that "fossils are made of rock so it's hard to break them". You can ask questions – and countless children have enjoyed being pictured by the giant fossilised leg. "It's a genuine Woolly Mammoth leg", says Jim. "It's 168cm tall, and was found on the seabed of the North Sea." Or maybe you'll be interested in the fossilised oysters that are known as devil's toenails – gross!

If you're on a pocket money budget, head for the **'fossils for £1'** table where someone recently found something that was so rare, that they wrote a four page scientific paper about it.

You can also enter the **free colouring competitions** - just pop in, pick up a picture, then drop it back later for judging (kids only, sorry Dad).

And finally… there's Jim's **'fossil of the week'** competition– just bring in any fossil you've found on your visit to the Isle of Wight. He'll identify your finds, and there is a prize each week for the best one brought in. Good luck, dinosaur hunters!

Jurassic Jim is the author of 'The Essential Guide to Fossiling on the Isle of Wight', on sale in the shop.

Jurassic Jim, 43 High Street, Shanklin, Isle of Wight PO37 6JJ
Tel: 01983 864577 jurassicjim.com

DINO DISCOUNTS

ISLE OF WIGHT Official Dinosaur Safari Guide

WORTH OVER £17

Come on kids, let's go!

DINOSAUR ISLE
ONE CHILD FREE WITH EACH FULL PAYING ADULT:

SAVE £4 PER CHILD ON ENTRY

dinosaurisle.com
Culver Parade, Sandown PO36 8QA

ISLAND GEMS FOSSIL AND GEM SHOP
10% OFF ALL PURCHASES. EQUIVALENT TO:

£2 OFF WHEN YOU SPEND £20

island-gems.co.uk
The Cottage, High Street, Godshill PO38 3HZ

REFLECTIONS FOSSIL, GEM & GIFT SHOP.
10% OFF ALL PURCHASES OVER £5. EQUIVALENT TO:

£2 OFF WHEN YOU SPEND £20

Find them on Facebook
1a Wheatsheaf Lane, Yarmouth PO41 0PF

BROWNS TEAROOM
10% OFF ALL FOOD & DRINK. EQUIVALENT TO:

£2 OFF ANY £20 FAMILY MEAL

brownsfamilygolf.com
Yaverland Road, Sandown PO36 8QA – near Dinosaur Isle

JURASSIC JIM FOSSIL & MINERAL SHOP.
20% OFF ALL PURCHASES. EQUIVALENT TO:

£4 OFF WHEN YOU SPEND £20

fossilshop.co.uk
43 High Street, Shanklin PO37 6JJ

CINDERELLA'S TEAROOM
20% OFF ALL DRINKS. EQUIVALENT TO:

£2 OFF WHEN YOU SPEND £10

cinderellas-lifestyle.com
7 High Street, Shanklin PO37 6JZ – near Jurassic Jim

DINOSAUR EXPEDITIONS, CONSERVATION AND PALAEOART CENTRE
10% OFF ANY ADMISSION. EQUIVALENT TO:

£1.10 OFF A FAMILY TICKET

dinosaurexpeditions.co.uk
Dinosaur Farm, Military Road, Brighstone PO30 4PG

Terms & conditions
• One voucher only per transaction. • Each voucher can only be used once. • Voucher cannot be used in conjunction with any other voucher, special offer, promotion or discount. • Voucher can be discontinued at the issuer's discretion. • Vouchers have no monetary value.

THE END...

© John Sibbick

So what happened to the Island's dinosaurs? Well, sadly they met a very watery end, around 115 million years ago.

After reigning for 25 million years, their paradise started to become submerged in water. Maybe the land surface sank, or the sea level rose – or perhaps it was a bit of both.

Whatever the reason, the result was that it became muddier, then sandier, and then chalkier, as the land was flooded by lagoons, then by shallow sea, and then by the deep ocean. The rocks here are proof of this. Fossils tell a similar tale, as the land-living animals were replaced by fresh-water creatures, and then sea life.

And that, as they say, is that. The end.

...OR IS THIS THE BEGINNING?

If you've enjoyed your dinosaur safari, this needn't be the end of the story. You can...

- Download Visit Isle of Wight's free Dino App and meet the virtual dinosaurs (see page 28).
- Go on a group fossil-hunting walk.
- Visit **Dinosaur Isle**, Europe's first purpose built dinosaur museum.
- Go to the **Dinosaur Expeditions, Conservation and Palaeoart Centre** to see amazing local finds.
- Visit the super-scary animatronic dinosaurs at **Blackgang Chine**.
- Read all about dinosaurs. The shops here have great books, including **Daisy and the Isle of Wight Dragon** by Martin Simpson.
- Go shopping for rare fossils and gems.

Dinosaur Expeditions, Conservation and Palaeoart Centre
Military Road, Brighstone, PO30 4PG.
Tel: 07837 728810 or 01983 740844
dinosaurexpeditions.co.uk

Dinosaur Isle
Culver Parade, Sandown, PO36 8QA.
Tel: 01983 404344 dinosaurisle.com

Island Gems
High Street, Godshill, PO38 3HZ.
Tel: 01983 740493 island-gems.co.uk

Jurassic Jim
43 High Street, Shanklin, PO37 6JJ.
Tel: 01983 864577 jurassicjim.com

Reflections
1a Wheatsheaf Lane, Yarmouth, PO41 0PF. Tel: 01983 760244
reflectionsisleofwight.co.uk

The Fossil Cavern
76A High St, Shanklin, PO37 6NJ.
Tel: 01983 868874 fossilcavern.co.uk

Neovenator – the fiercest known predator of the Early Cretaceous, reconstructed at Dinosaur Isle.

For more listings and contact details go to the 'Dinosaur Island' pages on the official Tourist Board website for the Island.

visitisleofwight.co.uk